P. de Villiers

The signature of Gutenberg

P. de Villiers

The signature of Gutenberg

ISBN/EAN: 9783337041724

Printed in Europe, USA, Canada, Australia, Japan

Cover: Foto ©ninafisch / pixelio.de

More available books at **www.hansebooks.com**

The Signature

of

Gutenberg

by

P. De Villiers, M.D.

London

Published by Kerby and Endean

190 Oxford Street

MDCCCLXXXIII

The Signature

of

Gutenberg

(Translation.)

THE GRAND DUCHY OF HESSE : MAYORALTY OF THE
PROVINCIAL-CAPITAL, MAINZ.

To P. DE VILLIERS, M.D.

WE have taken with pleasure the, to us, particularly
interesting communication of your agreeable letter of the
12th ult., that you have succeeded in discovering Gutenberg's subscription-signature of the year 1454, and that
you purpose dedicating the, on this account, forthcoming
work to the city of Mainz, which is indeed most closely
identified with the name of Gutenberg.

Now that the citizen representatives of this place have
declared themselves ready to accept with pleasure of this
dedication, we do not fail to express to you our thanks
for the proved attention to us, with the sincere wish that
your endeavours may be accompanied with the greatest
success.

Most respectfully,

DR. OESCHNER.

Nov. 29, 1877.

No. I.—See Page 25.

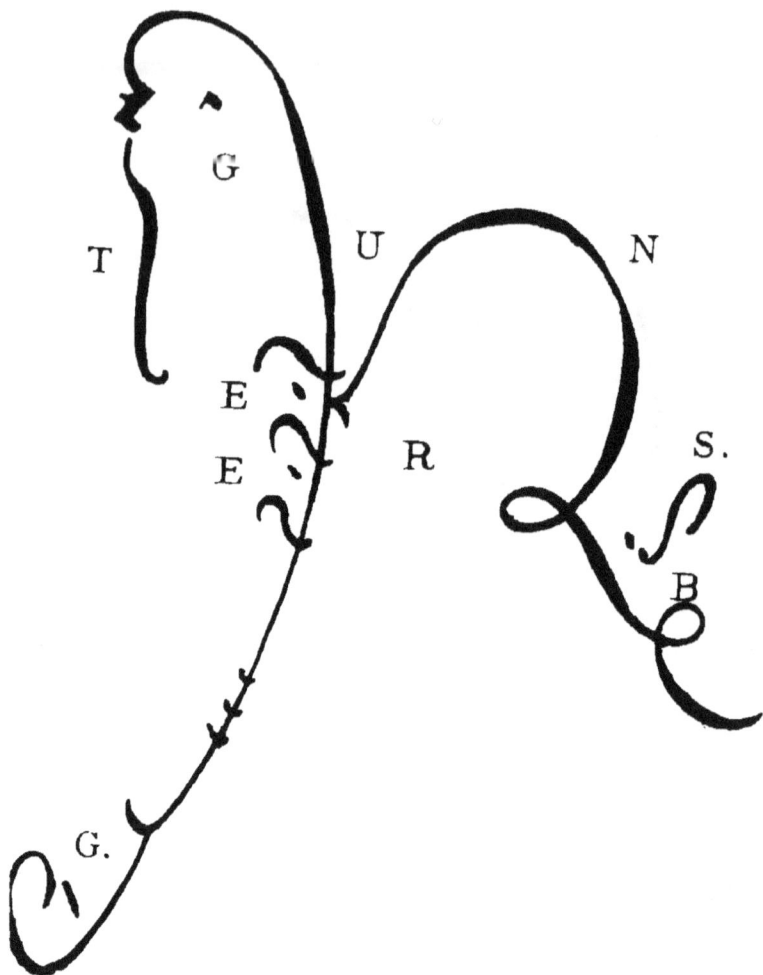

No. II.—See Page 25.

The Signature

of

Gutenberg

by

P. De Villiers, M.D.

London

Published by Kerby and Endean

190 Oxford Street

MDCCCLXXXVIII

LONDON: PRINTED BY KERBY AND ENDEAN, 190, OXFORD STREET.

Almæ Urbi Maguntinæ

nationis inclitæ germanicæ

quam Dei clementia tam alto ingenii lumine

donoque gratuito

cæteris terrarum nationibus præferre

illustrareque dignatus est

Johannes Gutenbergius

ut ipse scripsit

quum in illa cibitate

non calami stili aut pennæ suffragio

sed mira patronarum formarumque concordia

proportione et modulo

impressit atque confecit

Literas Indulgentiarum

Biblia Sacra

et

Catholicon

iste libellus

de

Chirographo

Gutenbergii

dicatur

Anno ab incarnatione Domini MDCCCXXVIII Anno a Manifestatione Dibina Artis Gutenbergianæ CCCCXXIV Egregia in Cibitate Londinensi ubi repertus est modus legendi Gutenbergii Chirographum a Petro de Villiers Doctore in Arte Medicali &c.

The Author desires to acknowledge his indebtedness to the Trustees and Librarians of the British Museum for the very kind and liberal way in which they placed the many valuable documents in this noble Institution at his service, and by which he was led, step by step, to this important discovery of the Signature of Gutenberg.

The Signature of Gutenberg.

I.

BEAUTIFUL Autographs are rare and curious, and are carefully sought after in the present day for many and good reasons. But sometimes it has happened that even clever amateurs possess them unconsciously, and without knowing their high historic value. Such a mischance has occurred with exceedingly interesting autographs, as, for example, Gutenberg's, the inventor of printing.

Up to this time no one, to our knowledge, has anywhere recognised a specimen of Gutenberg's handwriting, unless we accept the statement "that he rubricated with his own hand all the copies of the Bible of 1455," which is considered as his work by all bibliographers.*

But this is a statement only, an assertion without foundation : an opinion without value. Gutenberg was an impatient searcher, an indefatigable inventor, and not in the least a scribe, a rubricator, or an illuminator. Such an occupation would not have agreed with the man who had

---

* See the *Note* on *The Pretended Handwriting of Gutenberg.*

recently found out "the divine art of writing without employing a pen."

Such opinion may, then, be rejected without further investigation. But there is one fact worthy of special attention, and it is this, that the handwriting, or at least the signature of Gutenberg, exists only in a certain limited number of documents belonging to various persons, and the happy possessors have not, up to this day, seemed even to suspect it.

This appears at first sight to be remarkable. Thus the Marquis de Laborde, whose scientific and extraordinary sagacity in questions touching the origin of printing all bibliophiles acknowledge, and who has published a fac-simile of the signature here under consideration, had not been able to read it, and had only seen in it the flourish (*paraphe*) of an unknown hand.*

And, indeed, this signature seems to be nothing else than a flourish written at the back of the Letters of Indulgence, printed at Mentz in MCCCCLIV and MCCCCLV, by Gutenberg himself.

It contains his name in full, in the form of a monogram, perfectly legible to anyone acquainted with this style of monogrammatic signature, and which was much used by people of note in the twelfth, thirteenth, fourteenth, and fifteenth centuries.

---

* *Origines de l'Imprimerie à Mayence et à Bamberg*, par le Marquis de Laborde, in 4to., Paris, MDCCCXL.

II.

We will at first briefly recall some particulars respecting the Letters of Indulgence (*Literæ Indulgentiarum*), for such a digression is necessary to clearly establish the fact that we desire to demonstrate.

In the year MCCCCLIII Paolino Zappo,* counsellor and secretary to John de Lusignan, King of Cyprus, arrived in Italy with the mission for executing the orders contained in a Bull of Pope Nicholas V., permitting his sovereign to sell indulgences in Europe, for the purpose of organising a new crusade against the Moslems, who had recently seized Constantinople. It is well known that this traffic was one of the causes of the Reformation.

Zappo sent to Germany John de Castro, charged to represent him in the mission.

Printing was beginning to work at Mentz, and Gutenberg was preparing his first edition of the Bible. This new invention was destined to be a powerful auxiliary to the plentiful reproduction

---

* Mr. S. L. Sotheby (*Principia Typographica*, 3 vols., folio, London, MDCCCLVII) has partly re-established the name of Paolino Zappo, which had been Germanised, disfigured, and lately translated into Paul Chappe by the Marquis de Laborde. Zappo was a man of high distinction, entrusted all his life with delicate and important embassies. There exists still in the East a family of the same name; many of its members have been noted for their ability.

of Letters of Indulgence with economy. Mr.
Sotheby rightly thinks that the printing was, in
all probability, known only to the Legate who
issued them, and to the workmen who executed
them ; for they show many imperfections calculated to simulate the irregularity of handwriting.
Thus the lines are not of the same length, the
same letters present a great variety of forms, and
it might be supposed that they were not cast from
a matrix, but cut by hand.

No one seems to have suspected the way in
which these documents were made ; however, it
appears that there was a very extensive sale of
indulgences in some provinces of Germany. Up
to the present it has been thought that they have
not gone beyond that country, but this idea
is possibly incorrect, for an ancient and noble
Italian family possesses one of them, dated Pisa
MCCCCLV.

Two sorts of type were used for printing them :
the first of or about the dimension of double-
pica, the other smaller and less regular. The
first is identical with the type used by Gutenberg
in the composition of his Bible ; it is found, too,
in the *Donatus* of Fust and Schoffer. A variety
of the large types appears to have been used in
the Bible of Pfister. The small type is similar
in all the copies, but the capital letters constantly
engraved on wood show very great differences.

The Signature

of

Gutenberg

by

P. De Villiers, M.D.

London

Published by Kerby and Endean

190 Oxford Street

MDCCCLXXXVIII

LONDON: PRINTED BY KERBY AND ENDEAN, 190, OXFORD STREET.

The Letters of Indulgence are in thirty, thirty-two, and thirty-one lines. The text in each presents several variations.

The examination of these different conditions has led the Marquis de Laborde to classify them into three editions and five issues, as follows :—

1st edition : 30 lines $\begin{cases} \text{1st issue....MCCCCLIV.} \\ \text{2nd issue....MCCCCLV.} \end{cases}$

2nd edition : 32 lines—the only
issue ....MCCCCLIV.

3rd edition : 31 lines $\begin{cases} \text{1st issue....MCCCCLIV.} \\ \text{2nd issue....MCCCCLV.} \end{cases}$

The first copy known was discovered at the beginning of the last century by Hanselmann ; it is now in Lord Spencer's rich collection. Some years afterwards Schelhorn recognised its importance in the history of printing. Since that time a few others have been found, especially in bindings of old books, where they had been used as things without value.

Originally a seal was appended to them by a strip of parchment inserted in a horizontal opening cut in the lower part of the document. The following inscription can be read on the seal still attached to the copy belonging to Lord Spencer :—

S. Indulge'tiaru' a'plissimaru', pro deffe'sione fidei regi ciprie co'cessaru'.

All bibliographers agree in regarding the Letters of Indulgence as the first entirely typographic
work ever published ; however, considering the
variations of the text, and especially the simi-
larity of the type with that used in the Bible of
Pfister, some of them have seemed inclined to
think that, as early as MCCCCLIV, others beside
Gutenberg knew and practised the art of printing
in moveable letters.

That is a mistake. All the Letters of Indulgence were printed by Gutenberg, at Mentz, at
the date they bear, in full letters, in MCCCCLIV
and MCCCCLV. We now proceed to prove this
assertion.

III.

These Letters of Indulgence bear the signature
of Gutenberg, and it is the monogram that the
Marquis de Laborde thinks to be a *paraphe* (flourish) made by the Secretary to the King of Cyprus
or by his delegate.

How can the sense of so important a document,
and the reading, so easy, of the strokes constituting that so-called *paraphe*, have escaped such
a learned man and other amateurs who have had
it, or still have it, in their hands ? This is difficult
of explanation, unless we suppose (which is quite
natural) that they have been exclusively preoccu-

pied with the typographic question, on which their attention has been entirely concentrated.

The Marquis de Laborde evidently has only carefully scrutinised the printed document, comparing it with others of the same kind, and drawn from his inquiries the right conclusion as to other matters, to which he has adhered.

He has also proved the existence of the *paraphe* on the back of all the copies, although the parchment had been often scraped for use in binding. He was not, however, able to decipher the so-called *paraphe*.

But this proof is a precious fact, because it demonstrates that Gutenberg, who could not print his name in full on documents destined to be sold as manuscripts, intended at least to put his mark, to fix the trace of his discovery, and to place his seal in such a manner on each of them, in order that some day his name should be read in these bold and proud strokes: a noble ambition, if ever there were one, and a legitimate pride.

It may be an objection that, since he signed the Letters of Indulgence, why did he not sign his Bible also, that magnificent and imperishable monument of his genius of which a complete re-production, worthy of him, is preparing at the present moment ? *

---

* See the *Appendix* concerning the Biblia Sacra Gutenbergiana, and the reproduction of this book in fac-simile.

To this objection we will simply answer, that none can know whether Gutenberg has signed his Bible typographically or in another manner In deed it is a fact that, at the very moment when he was ready to issue his great work, he was obliged, by an iniquitous lawsuit, to abandon his printing works, his books, all the materials for his labour and production, to Fust, his partner. If then the Bible had been signed by him, Fust could easily have suppressed the signature of the master; furthermore, he must have done so with a view to purely mercantile speculation, since he sold the greater part of the copies as real manuscripts. Besides, it was necessary to efface every trace which would substantiate Gutenberg's claim to the invention. All these causes probably operated to deprive the said Bible of the mark or the monogram of Gutenberg. The only strokes of his handwriting actually known are found on the Letters of Indulgence.

IV.

Several documents combine to establish the fact that Hans Gensfleisch, of Sulgeloch, of Gutenberg was the inventor of printing. His monogram contains in full the noble name of Gutenberg, under which he was designated and known by his contemporaries, and also by the use of the initial letter of the name of Sulgeloch. Trithcim, who received from Schoffer details of his life, which he has transmitted to us, gives him always the name of Gutenberg, citizen of Mentz.

Like many monograms of the same period, the one before us seems, at first sight, rather confused, but it becomes clear and readable when it is studied on the simple plan of examining each letter apart, and then combining the whole.

It is easy, by glancing at the fac-simile which accompanies this work, to perceive at once that the first stroke presents the form of a G much curved in its inferior part. It is the initial of the name. At the foot of this capital letter the curve just pointed out is doubled by the addition of a similar curve, forming a second G. This is perfectly conformable with the rules of what we will call monogrammic writing, in which a simple stroke often indicates a repetition of the same letter. We shall show hereafter another example.

The principal letter, G, is barred at about the half of its length by three thick strokes projecting on the left into the interior of the letter, and separated from each other by two smaller oblique strokes. These are two E E, placed inversely, in order not to interfere with the great stroke on the right, which composes other letters.

A vertical stroke, strongly inflected at top and bottom, starts from underneath the upper of the

G. This is a T perfectly clear, in German writing of the period.

Thus we already possess G G, E E, T. The reading of the rest now becomes easy. The whole, indeed, at the first glance presents the figure of an R. But just where the second small stroke approaches the descending line of the G, V as in ancient, or U as in modern writing, can be seen without difficulty.

From the middle of the great perpendicular stroke starts a curved line, which takes the form of N, and is prolonged into an R, of which the termination is twice curved. This double curve, in turning the figure upside down, indicates the principal part of a B, in the middle of which is an S, accompanied by a thick point.

Thus, to the letters already read, two G's, two E's, and a T we may now add R, U, N, B, and thus possess all the letters constituting the name of GUTENBERG.

We have in addition an S, which is the initial of the name of Sulgeloch.

This cannot be reproached with being a fanciful interpretation, but it is presented in order perfectly logical, and preserves the mysterious character which Gutenberg evidently wished to give to his signature.

In fact, when we commence the preceding examination we are at once struck by the initial letter of the name, G ; the second letter, U, presents itself afterwards without possible hesitation. But as the G cannot be read without attention being called to the appended T, which accompanies it, the two E E which cross it, we are almost involuntarily obliged to read them, and thus to insert the first in its proper place, between the T and the N. The following letter N is immediately seen then, including the second syllable, TEN. We must necessarily stop there, for B and R cannot be read without the help of a vowel. The idea comes naturally to insert the second E between these two letters; next to which the second G, indicated at the bottom of the initial, finds then its use as final.

As to the S, the point which accompanies it shows it is an isolated letter.*

V.

The progressive order of this reasoning, we have seen, is logical ; the result of our analysis sufficiently demonstrates the fact.

This monogram is, therefore, without doubt, the signature of Gutenberg. No other hand but his own could have written such an assemblage

---

* The form of this letter might contribute to have it mistaken for a J, initial of Johannes, which is a Latin translation of Hans. We were in some doubt, but we believe we are right in adhering to the reading we have given above.

of letters as compose his name.   We have already shown the reasons for this statement.

The authenticity of the document is not a subject of doubt.   This monogram has always existed upon all the Letters of Indulgence of this period. Others before us have seen, copied, and repro- duced it : we claim no other merit than that of having been *the first to decipher it.*

Whence one may conclude that we really possess the true signature of Gutenberg on each of the copies of the first printed work coming from his hands before the completion of the great Bible of MCCCCLV.

APPENDIX.

BIBLIA SACRA

Ut primum metallicis typis edita a JOHANNE GUTEN-BERGIO,—*Maguntiae, A.D. Mcccclv,—hodie rediviva cura et sumptibus Bibliophilorum et* PETRI DE VILLIERS, M.D.

THE origin of Printing is surrounded with a certain obscurity; but two facts are none the less well established, namely, that John Gutenberg was the inventor of the Typographic art, and that the first great work printed by him is the fine EDITIO PRINCEPS of the Holy Bible published at Mainz in 1455.

This undated Latin Bible is in the form of a large folio. Her Majesty Queen Victoria is in possession of a superb copy which we have been able to examine and consult; the British Museum exhibits another (King's Library, Case III. No. 1) among the books destined to form a history of the origin and progress of typography; it is on vellum, and thus catalogued :—

" C. g. a. s.—Bible, in Latin.—Begin. [With the prologus of Saint Jerome.]—[F]Unter ambrosius tua michi munuscula p-ferens detulit sml et suabissimus literas: etc.] Genesis begins Fol. 5, recto, col. 1 at the top :—[J]N principio crcabit deus celu' et terra'.]—End. Folio 641 verso, col. 2. [Gratia dn'i n'ri ihesu cu' omnibs bobis amc'.] G.L.—ED.PR. [p. Gutenberg. Mentz, MCCCCL-LV?] fol. Nota.—The earliest printed book known, commonly called the Mazarine Bible, because the copy which first attracted notice in modern times was discovered in the library of Cardinal Mazarine. Without title-page, pagination, or signatures; 641 leaves, printed in double columns, 42 lines to a full column ; the initials and rubrics are in MS. throughout."

The date of the impression of this Bible cannot be
open to the least doubt; it is determined by the
manuscript note inserted in one of the copies of the
Richelieu Library, at Paris—a note written in red
ink at the end of the second volume, in these words :

" Iste liber illuminatus ligatus et completus est per Henricum
Cremer vicarium ecclesie collegiate sancti Maguntini Stephani sub
anno Domini millesimo quadringentesimo quinquagesimo sexto
festo Assumptionis gloriose Virginis. Deo gratias. Alleluia."

Now, in the preceding year—1455—Gutenberg, it
is well known, finished the impression of the Bible ;
he broke off his connection with Fust on the 6th of
November in the same year ; the date is therefore
certain.   The Bible illuminated, bound, and corrected
by Henry Cremer could not have been published later
than 1455.

Such is the abridged history of the book which we
now reproduce in its entirety.   The number of copies
known to be in existence at the present day is very
limited ; and their worth is above all estimation.   It
augments with the lapse of time, and amateurs cannot
procure them at any price.

Even the reproduction of a small specimen of this
work has scarcely been attempted up to the present—
a work so great from the genius of which it gives
proof, so interesting for the history of the art which
has the most contributed to the progress of civilisa-
tion, so curious from the Christian point of view,
since it was the first public manifestation of the Holy
Scriptures, and has served for type to all the repro-
ductions which have been made of them.

In this last respect the Bible of Gutenberg is an
interesting subject of study ; the text it contains has
been modified, the arrangement of contents altered,

and certain parts of the work suppressed. It repro-
duces the Bible as it was read in the Middle Ages, in
the manuscript copies.

Such are the principal points to bring under the
notice of men skilled in the study of the Holy Scriptures, as also of amateur collectors of rare books.
They will find in our reproduction ample matter to
satisfy their science and curiosity. On the other hand,
literary men can profit by it to familiarise themselves
with the reading of the ancient texts and editions of
the fifteenth century, which present very great ana-
logies with the writing of the manuscripts which pre-
ceded them.

A similar publication appeared to us to recommend
itself especially to the attention of our age, which is
so occupied with questions of religious erudition.

The Bible of Gutenberg is composed of six hundred
and forty-one leaves; it is printed in two columns,
each containing forty-two lines; the height of the
columns is ten inches and three-quarters, and the
size of the type corresponds with that of the double-
pica of modern printers.

The letters are gothic; the sheets have neither
signatures, catch-words, nor pagination; the capitals
are made by hand; and the rubrics and the headings
of the different books are in red. The work has no
title-page, and is generally divided into two volumes.

Our reproduction will be entirely conformable with
this description. We shall add to it two title-pages
printed in the same style.

A certain number of sheets placed at the end, and
printed also in gothic type, will contain :—1st. An
Index of the various Readings. 2nd. The History of
the Book. 3rd. The List of Subscribers.

Every Subscriber will receive a *testimonial* stating

the share he has had in the execution of this monument of the Christian Faith, and in the reproduction of this *chef d'œuvre* of typographic art, which owes to this belief its first and its finest manifestation.

The work will be privately printed for Subscribers only.

THE CATHOLICON.

In the year MCCCCLX was published the Catholicon, by John Balbi, of Genoa (*de Janua*), the only important work produced by Gutenberg, when he succeeded in establishing a new printing press at Mentz. This splendid volume, large folio, contains 375 sheets printed in large type, in two columns of sixty-six lines each, without numbers, catch-words, or signatures. The initials have been omitted in the press, and painted by hand.

The printer has signed this book with a subscription of a very high interest; he has condensed in a few lines the history of his invention, and he has attributed his discovery to a divine inspiration.

We transcribe it in full :—

" Altissimi presidio cujus nutu infantium lingue fiunt diserte, quique nimio sepe parbulis rebelat quod sapientibus celat, hic liber egregius Catholicon, dominice Incarnacionis anni MCCCCLX, alma in urbe Maguntina nacionis inclite germanice, quam Dei clementis tam alto ingenii lumine, donoque gratuito, ceteris terrarum nationibus preferre, illustrareque dignatus es, non calami, stili aud penne suffragio, sed mira patronarum, formarumque concordia proporcione et modulo impressus atque confectus est.

" Hinc tibi, sancte Pater, Nato cum Flamine sacro,
    Laus et honor Domino trino tribuatur et uno.
    Ecclesie laudi libro hoc catholice plaude,
    Qui laudare piam semper non linque Mariam.

" DEO GRACIAS."

THE LETTER OF INDULGENCE.

UNIVERSIS Cristi fidelibus presentes litteras inspecturis PAULINUS CHAPPE, Consiliarius, Ambasiator et procurator generalis Serenissimi Regis Cipri in hac parte, Salutem in domino. Cum Sanctissimus in Cristo pater et dominus noster dominus Nicolaus, divina providentia papa V, Afflictioni Regni Cipri, misericorditer compatiens contra perfidissimos crucis cristi hostes Teucros et Saracenos, gratis concessit omnibus cristi fidelibus ubi libet constitutis, ipsos per aspersionem sanguinis domini nostri jhesu cristi pie exhortando, qui, intra triennium a prima die Maii Anno Domini Mcccclii incipiendum, pro defensione catholice fidei et Regni predicti, de facultatibus suis magis vel minus, pro ut ipsorum videbitur conscientiis, procuratoribus vel nunciis Substitutis pie erogaverint, ut Confessores ydonei seculares vel Regulares per ipsos eligendi, confessionibus eorum auditis, pro commissis etiam Sedi Apostolice reservatis excessibus, criminibus atque delictis quantumcunque gravibus, pro una vice tantum, debitam absolutionem impendere et penitentiam salutarem injungere. Nec non si id humiliter patierint, ipsos a quibuscunque excommunicationum, suspensionum et Interdicti Aliisque sententiis, censuris et penis ecclesiasticis a Jure vel ab homine promulgatis, quibus forsan innodati existunt, absolvere; Injuncta pro modo culpa penitentia salutari vel aliis que de Jure fuerint injungenda Ac eis vere penitentibus et confessis. Vel si forsan propter amissionem loquele confiteri non poterint, signa contritionis ostendendo plenissimam omnium peccatorum suorum de quibus ore confessi et corde contriti fuerint. Indulgentiam ac plenariam remissionem semel in vita et semel in mortis articulo ipsis auctoritate Apostolica

concedere valeant. Satisfactione per eos facta si
supervixerint aut per eorum heredes si tunc transie-
rint, Sic tamen quod post indultum concessum, por
unum annum singulis sextis feriis vel quadam alia
die jejunent, legitimo impedimento ecclesie precepto
Regulari observantia penitentia injuncta, voto vel
alias, non obstante. Et ipsis impedimentis in dicto
anno vel ejus parte, Anno sequenti vel alias quam
primum poterint jejunabunt. Et si in aliquo annorum
vel eorum parte dictum jejunium commode adimplere
nequiverint, Confessor ad id electus in alia commutare
poterit caritatis opera, que ipsi facere etiam teneantur,
Dummodo tum ex confidentia remissionis hujusmodi,
quod absit, peccare non presumant : Alioquin dicta
concessio quo ad plenariam remissionem in mortis
articulo et remissio quo ad peccata ex confidentia, ut
premittitur, commissa, nullius sint roboris vel mo-
menti. Et quia devoti_____ Juxta dictum indultum de facultatibus suis pie eroga_____ merito
hujusmodi indulgentiis gaudere debet. In veritatis
testimonium Sigillum ad hoc ordinatum presentibus
Litteris testimonialibus est appensum. Datum_____

FORMA PLENISSIME ABSOLUTIONIS ET REMISSIONIS IN VITA.

MISEREATUR TUI, etc., Dominus noster ihesus
Cristus per suam sanctissimam et piissimam mise-
ricordiam te absolvat Et auctoritate ipsius Beatorum-
que petri et pauli Apostolorum ejus ac Auctoritate
Apostolica mihi commissa et tibi concessa, Ego te
absolvo ab omnibus peccatis tuis, contritis, confessis
et oblitis, Etiam ab omnibus casibus, excessibus,
criminibus atque delictis quantumcunque gravibus,
Sedi Apostolice reservatis, Nec non a quibuscunque

excommunicationum, suspensionum et interdicti aliisque sentenciis, censuris et penis ecclesiasticis e Jure vel ab homine promulgatis, si quas incurristi, dando tibi plenissimam omnium peccatorum tuorum indulgentiam et remissionem In quantum claves sancte matris ecclesie in hac parte se extendunt. In nomine patris et filii et spiritus sancti. Amen.

FORMA PLENARIE REMISSIONIS IN MORTIS ARTICULO.

MISEREATUR TUI, etc., Dominus noster ut supra. Ego te absolvo ab omnibus peccatis tuis contritis, confessis et oblitis, restituendo te unitati fidelium et sacramentis ecclesie, Remittendo tibi penas purgatorii quas propter culpas et offensas incurristi, dando tibi plenariam omnium peccatorum tuorum remissionem, In quantum claves sancte matris ecclesie in hac parte se extendunt. In nomine patris et filii et spiritus sancti. Amen.

THE TWO SIGNATURES OF GUTENBERG.

WE give at the back of our fac-simile of the Letter of Indulgence two slightly different monograms or signatures of Gutenberg, taken from two documents. Number I. can be seen on application to the Author ; Number II. is the fac-simile of the signature that is on the Letter of Indulgence found by Hanselmann, and published by the Marquis de Laborde. It can be seen at the first sight that they have been written by hand, by the same hand, and not printed from a block, as might have been supposed if one only had been placed before our readers.

THE PRETENDED HANDWRITING OF GUTENBERG.

WE find in the library catalogue of Mr. Quaritch, London, page 1378, No. 17,545, the following note :—

"GUTTENBERG's MAZARINE BIBLE, 2 vols., large stout folio, *the original and genuine issue of the book, printed on Paper, as distinguished from the second issue made by Fust and Schöffer, to which all the copies on vellum belong.*

"A PERFECT AND EXTRAORDINARY FINE COPY

of the full size, most of the leaves being rough and UNCUT, *so as even to show the ancient MS. signatures and chapter-numbers, as written down by* GUTTENBERG *himself for the guidance of the binder and illuminator.* . . .

"One of the most remarkable books in existence, as being the first great effort of the Printing Press (known as the *Mazarine Bible,* because the copy in the Mazarine Library possesses the MS. subscription by the illuminator, which fixes the date of the book). . . .

"Two sorts of copies of the Mazarine Bible are met with. The first is the issue by Guttenberg himself, probably in 1455, of which no copy on vellum is known ; and the second is the issue made by Fust in or after 1456, when he had legally robbed the Inventor of his whole stock of types and copies. It is to this second issue that all the vellum copies (and also *most* of the paper copies) belong. The variation between the two issues is easily distinguished ; in the second, or what we may call the vellum sort, the first five leaves, as well as one at the beginning of Maccabees, were reprinted so as to occupy, by the means of newly-cut types of abbreviations, only FORTY LINES per column instead of FORTY-TWO, as in the original book. It is to be presumed that those leaves were spoiled in the transfer of the stock to Fust ; the reason why he did not reprint them in exact conformity cannot be ascertained. It might have been a vain desire to display fresh additions to the old type, which had been cast by Schoeffer for him after the severance from Guttenberg ; it might have been to make the Bible seem a different edition. WHATEVER WAS THE CAUSE, THE FACT REMAINS, AND WE ARE ENABLED THEREFORE TO CLAIM A SUPERIORITY AND PRIORITY FOR THE UNMIXED ISSUE ON PAPER, OVER ALL THE COPIES ON VELLUM. The distinction may be marked in terms by speaking of the Perkin's Bible on Paper as—

"(1) The Mazarine Bible, First Issue, by Guttenberg ; and the one on vellum as—

"(2) The Mazarine Bible, Second and Altered Issue, by Fust and Schoeffer.

"We doubt if the copy above described can be rivalled by any other in existence, for condition and size. It fulfils every requirement of the most fastidious collector, being perfect, clean, and for the most part uncut, as well as containing a brilliant and fine impression of the text. Even the MS. memoranda of signatures, and numbers of chapters, still remain at foot and on the margins of the pages, being unquestionably in the handwriting of Guttenberg himself. . ."

This note contains nearly as many blunders as phrases : we will mention only the principal.

(1) The name of Gutenberg is written with one T only. Guttenberg, or Guttemberg, as written by many foreign bibliographers, is not correct according to the German orthograph.

(2) The Mazarine Bible, bearing the manuscript subscription which determines its date, is not in the Mazarine Library, but in the Richelieu Library.

(3) Two sorts of copies of this Bible are met with, one on vellum, the other on paper. The first is in every respect preferable to the other. The abbreviations are the same in both kinds, and as to the differences in the composition and in the number of lines, they are to be found in copies of each sort. This observation may be applied to nearly all the first books printed ; for example, to the *Psalterium* of MCCCCLVIII. Mr. Quaritch's Bible is in no way an exception. Thus the two pretended editions are really but one, and that one is the work of Gutenberg.

(4) Gutenberg is not, and cannot be, the author of the manuscript notes set forth on the Bible offered for sale by Mr. Quaritch. Indeed, some similar annotations can be seen on all the copies now known, and it cannot be admitted that Gutenberg annotated all with his own hand, thus performing the office of scribe and rubricator upon several hundred folio volumes of more than six hundred pages each, and at the same time their printer. There is another

reason more peremptorily demonstrating that it is useless to seek for a specimen of his handwriting in such a manner. Mr. Brunet, who could not foresee the extraordinary discovery (!) of Mr. Quaritch, has noticed in the copies belonging to the libraries of Munich and Vienna four sheets more than in the others, and "these sheets contain an index of summaries and chapters of the Bible for the special use of the illuminator who had to write those summaries."* Thus Gutenberg, having printed that index, had no occasion to do work which he intended providing for the scribes in his employment.

Finally, it is sufficient, since we have established the authenticity and *modus legendi* of the signature of Gutenberg, to compare the strokes which constitute that monogram with the above-mentioned annotations, to be persuaded without hesitation that they have not been written by the same hand.

We are very sorry indeed to destroy the illusions of a learned man who has been mistaken *bonâ fide;* but we have been compelled to do so in the interests of bibliographic science and truth.

---

* BRUNET, *Manuel du Libraire et de l'Amateur de Livres*, page 867 col. 1, in 8vo. Paris, MDCCCLX.

Index.

❖

NEW BOOKS RECENTLY PUBLISHED

BY

KERBY & ENDEAN.

THE HISTORY OF COACHES.

By G. A. Thrupp. Demy 8vo., beautifully illustrated, cloth, 6s.

"The volume is specially interesting to coach-builders, to antiquaries, and to anyone who wishes to know how the world has moved in the last four or five thousand years."—*Glasgow Herald.*

"Is an important volume, an almost exhaustive book of reference on the subject of coaches."—*Christian World.*

"A survey at once historical and artistic of carriages and carriage-building, from the dawn of history till now, . . . a volume for the coach-builder in the first instance, is rich in rare antiquarian details, set off by curious illustrations—a book of equal interest to the lover of old fashions, or the practical student of modern industries."—*Graphic.*

LAPLAND LIFE ;

Or, Summer Adventures in the Arctic Regions. By the Rev. Donald D. Mackinnon, M.A., Curate of Quebec Chapel. With Map and Illustrations, crown 8vo., cloth, 5s.

LAS MEMORIAS AND OTHER POEMS.

By A. F. A. W. Crown 8vo., cloth, 6s.

LENDING UNTO THE LORD;

Or, Three Days in the Life of Christian Fürchtegott Gellert, Poet and Professor in Leipsic University. By BARON CONWAY and J. RUSSELL ENDEAN. Illustrated from original designs by the Hon. CHARLOTTE ELLIS. Royal 16mo., 3s.

"I hope 'Lending unto the Lord' will have the good effect of recommending the duty of Christian benevolence which it inculcates."—*Abp. of Canterbury.*

"An important work, which the Archbishop hopes to read with the attention which it deserves."—*Abp. of York.*

"Dear Sir,—I thank you much for sending me a copy of your beautiful little work, 'Lending unto the Lord.' It is fitted to encourage such lending as, I fear, is too rare ; and, independently of this, to interest and please thoughtful Christian minds and hearts. Very truly yours, John Cumming. To J. Russell Endean, Esq."—*Rev. John Cumming, D.D., F.R.S.E.*

"It is a delightful little book."—*Rev. Donald Fraser, D.D.*

"'Lending unto the Lord' is an interesting book. It is nicely written, and ought to prove popular in the circle of readers to whom it is addressed."—*Athenæum.*

"'Lending unto the Lord' is a good book. The story brought the water into our eyes as we read it. It ought to sell by thousands. The narrative is calculated to foster that spirit of benevolence which is the glory of Christianity."—*Sword and Trowel.*

DAILY DEVOTION;

Or, Prayers Framed on the Successive Portions of the New Testament as Appointed in the New Lectionary, to which are added Forms of Prayer for a Fortnight, for Family or Private Use. By DANIEL MOORE, M.A., Chaplain in Ordinary to the Queen, and Vicar of Holy Trinity, Paddington. Large crown 8vo., cloth, 6s.

"This book provides a prayer suitable for family worship for every morning and evening of the year, and there is added a Form for Family Devotion for a Fortnight."—*English Churchman.*

"An excellent compilation. This useful Manual of Daily Devotion is admirably adapted for family or private use."—*Court Journal.*

www.ingramcontent.com/pod-product-compliance
Lightning Source LLC
Chambersburg PA
CBHW021452090426
42739CB00009B/1724